HORSES

HORSES

Michael Clayton

SMITHMARK

First published in the United States in 1992
by SMITHMARK Publishers Inc.,
16 East 32nd Street, New York, NY 10016

in association with Reed Consumer Books
a division of Reed International Books Limited

Reprinted 1992

ISBN 0-8317-4597-5

SMITHMARK books are available for bulk purchase for sales
promotion and premium use. For details write or telephone
the Manager of Special Sales, SMITHMARK Publishers Inc.,
16 East 32nd Street, New York, NY 10016; (212) 532-6600.

Printed in China

CONTENTS

EARLY DAYS

The wonderful world of horses is immensely varied.
As you will see in these pages, it is a world full of grace
and power. Horsemen pursue widely different
enthusiasms, but they a share basic concern for the
welfare of their horses and ponies, no matter how
differently they are bred.

Foals are born after a pregnancy of 11 months.
Their birth is planned for the spring, for that is when
the grass contains most nutrients to benefit the mare
and her offspring. The foal is capable of standing
within an hour of birth, and will very soon be able to
trot or even canter. Horses and ponies are creatures of
flight: their only defence against an attacker. Nature
intends the foal to flee from danger with its mother.
Understanding this factor is a key to using horse
psychology effectively in training. The horse's
extraordinary memory is another basic characteristic.

Although usually hardy, mares and foals raised
domestically need constant attention and vigilance.
If health problems do occur, they appear rapidly and
require instant action. The rewards can be immense
financially in Thoroughbred breeding, but whether it is
to be a racehorse or the smallest child's pony, the
arrival of a foal is always a miracle to be treasured.

Playful and boisterous as a foal may appear, it
relies heavily on its mother: the bond between
mare and foal is immensely strong. They should
never be out of each other's sight until the foal is
weaned at the age of about six months. If they are
separated accidentally, such as one getting the wrong
side of a fence, the mare and foal will ignore all
obstacles in order to rejoin, sometimes with dire
results. Eternal vigilance is therefore necessary for the
stud manager, especially on studs producing
Thoroughbreds, which are more volatile than their
more plebeian cousins.

Horses start Flat racing as two-year-olds but they are
still immature. A horse does not reach full maturity
until it is five years old, or even older: steeplechasers
and cross-country horses are not usually at their best
until well over seven years.

Heading for vastly different roles in the horse world: the comfortable piebald mare and her foal at home in their meadow, and the top-class Thoroughbred mare and her grey foal disporting themselves on the blue grass of Kentucky. The piebald pair are strong and hardy, probably of most use in harness, since they are wide across the wither, the area at the top of the shoulder.

Piebalds and skewbalds, brown and white, are often seen among the cobs and ponies still employed by some people to pull their carts and wagons. Horse colours often indicate their temperament and these are noted for their calm, tractable disposition. The Thoroughbreds in Kentucky are finer in build, but they are bred for toughness as well as speed, to withstand racing on America's demanding all-weather 'dirt' racecourses.

Running in a wild setting as a herd (previous pages), mares and foals will act in concert in moving across country. Although they prefer to keep out of trouble, mares can be extraordinarily aggressive in protecting foals, using their teeth to bite or their heels to deliver kicks. Mares with foals at foot must always be approached with caution in any setting.

Horses thrive best on grazing land containing bone-enriching calcium. They do not need the lush, wet, low-lying pasture land used for dairy cattle. From birth the horse can survive and flourish out of doors in all weathers, and a wide range of temperatures, provided it has sufficient room to find new grazing naturally. When we keep horses indoors and endeavour to turn them into competitive athletes or heavy workers, we change their diet drastically from grass to dry foods such as hay, corn and bran. We also ask them to adjust from the freedom of the herd pictured here to the restricted regime of stable life. It works, but it requires skill and understanding to make the best of a horse when it faces such a major change of lifestyle.

Horses will lie down to rest only when they feel secure. They are capable of standing for many hours, and will doze on their feet rather than risk being surprised or frightened while lying down. When grazing in groups some horses will always remain standing while others lie down. Countless centuries of breeding and domestication by humans have not eradicated such instincts.

Although as brave as a lion in tackling fearsome jumps, a horse is as timid as a mouse when confronted by an unusual object, however small. A horse which will take on a steeplechase course may easily be frightened by a paper bag blowing in its path while exercising.

And how horses love the sun on their backs, especially those with Thoroughbred bloodlines, which go back to the Arabs and Barbs of the Middle East.

PONY POWER

What a versatile and delightful breed is the Welsh
pony. It is marvellous as a distinctive breed, and also
mixes well with Arab or Thoroughbred blood to
produce splendid show and performance ponies.
Welsh ponies are among the glories of our equine
heritage, and are justifiably the object of much pride in
their native principality.
For riding or driving, the Welsh pony exhibits vitality,
athleticism and endurance. It is noted for its
intelligence too. The breed comes in four types, and
the pair seen here providing mutual back scratching –
with their teeth – are Welsh Section B. They are up to
13.2 hands in height and make ideal quality riding
ponies. The smaller type, Section A, is the pretty Welsh
mountain pony, up to 12 hands, often a child's first
pony. Sections C and D are Welsh ponies of cob type,
up to 13.2 hands and above that height, respectively.

The Haflingers cavorting in the snow are a mountain breed originating in the Austrian Tyrol. Although seldom higher than 14.2 hands the Haflinger is exceptionally strong, and is an ideal riding or driving breed.

The Shetland pony mare and foal (above) are members of the smallest of Britain's nine native breeds of pony, being up to 106cm (42 in) at the wither. They were used in the past as crofters' pack ponies in their native Shetland Isles. Nowadays they are firmly established as favourites among children's ponies.

For sheer impudence it would be hard to beat the Shetland pony. The Shetland Grand National has become an established favourite at horse shows. Here, the youthful riders and their mounts are delighting the crowd at the annual Royal Show at Stoneleigh, Warwickshire. They parade before the race, just like racehorses, and then set off at a gallop over a course of brush fences. Not a little of the fun is occasioned by the smallest pony in the race, which is inclined to miss out most of the fences and then join in the finish. It is all accompanied by a breathless Grand-National-style commentary on the public-address system.

T hose of us lucky enough as children to have ridden New Forest ponies know just how suitable they are for the young rider: sensible temperament, hardy, and a useful shape – narrow across the wither. They are from 12 to 14.2 hands. The group seen left are in woodland, but much of their native New Forest is moorland too. The ponies pastured nowadays in the Forest, Crown land since Norman times, belong to local people, who have commoners' rights. Disputes affecting these rights are still decided by the ancient Verderers' Court, and supervision of the ponies is exercised by four officers of the Court, known as Agisters.

Go to Devon to find Dartmoor ponies, seen above in their native setting, but, as with the New Forest breed, the best examples are to be found in private studs rather than living wild. The Dartmoor is smaller, up to 12.2 hands, and is an agile but tractable pony. It is immensely strong and can carry either small adults or children.

^AROUND THE WORLD

Even a heavy horse can raise a canter, as the Shire
horse (above) demonstrates while relaxing out at
grass. This is one of the glories of the British breeds,
and it is increasingly sought by buyers throughout the
world. The Shire's ancestors were the 'great horses' of
medieval times. In Britain Shires still work on the land
on a few farms where the old ways are cherished,
while in the cities they pull brewers' drays.
Another heavy horse (opposite), the Percheron, hails
from the La Perche district in France, and has Arab
blood far back in its breeding. It is used in harness
work all over the world. This horse is kept at the
famous Kentucky Horse Park at Lexington, Kentucky.

Y ou do not have to be an expert to guess that a horse is probably an Appaloosa. Just look for the spots. These distinctively marked and highly popular saddle-horses are descendants of horses taken to America by the Spanish *conquistadores* in the 16th century. Their name is derived from the Palouse Valley in Idaho, where they were bred by the Nez Percé Indians.

Do not imagine that they owe their popularity just to a fad because of their colour. They are good riding horses, and nowadays are also to be found in Europe, Australia and other countries. Not all spotted horses are Appaloosas. There are six pattern types permissible in the breed, and they often have vertically striped hooves. The Appaloosa is a compact horse, up to 15.2 hands.

The Selle Français
(French Saddle-
horse) is a term
used for cross-bred riding
horses in France, derived
from the old Norman
horse. English
Thoroughbred blood was
used to improve the
breed, and Arab stallions
were also used to breed
with French mares.
Thanks to their tote
system of betting on
horse-racing, the French
acquire large sums of
money for breeding all
types of horses, and they
do so very efficiently in
state-subsidized studs.

The Selle Francais is
classified in different
categories according to
height and weight. It is a
good quality hunter type
and exceedingly useful in
a wide variety of horse
sports other than racing.
They may be any colour,
but like this horse, a great
many are chestnut.

No other breed has had more influence on horse breeding throughout the world than the Arab. The desert tribes of Arabia developed the breed to suit their needs in battle, in transport, and as a friend and companion. The Prophet Mohammed himself declared that special care of horses should be an article of faith. These horses, above, are stabled in Morocco and are well suited to the extremes of heat in the Middle East, but the Arab horse has proved that it can thrive everywhere.

Arab blood was among the Eastern lines used to create the British Thoroughbred in the 17th and 18th centuries. In the 19th century the British imported Arab horses, which they valued highly as a separate breed, so the distinctive Arab is to be found looking over many a British loosebox.

'The purest and most beautiful of the equine races . . .' that is the claim made for the Arab horse by its fervent admirers, and it would be hard to dispute. The Arab has a distinctive head, tending to be 'dished', or concave, in profile, with a broad forehead tapering to a fine muzzle. The Arab's body is deep and roomy, and its back is short and level. Watch an Arab in movement, and you will see it carrying its tail in a characteristically high position. The good Arab horse seems to dance along in a floating motion. Yet this is no mere pretty horse; the Arab is justly renowned for its intelligence and its hardiness.

Its limbs are of especially fine but dense bone. Arab sheikhs who have become oil-rich in the postwar years have invested heavily in raising standards of Arab horse breeding higher than ever. The international market in Arab horses is big business, particularly as these horses are especially suitable for the growing sport of endurance riding.

More horse magic from the Middle East. The Barb, whose handsome head is seen on the left, is a breed hailing originally from Morocco and Algeria. They were taken to Spain by Muslim invaders in the eighth century, and from Spain they were transported to South America by the *conquistadores*. British horsemen fell in love with the Arabian breeds in the 17th century and Barbs were brought to England to be mixed with riding horses. They played their part in the development of the Thoroughbred, although not to the same extent as the pure-bred Arab.

The Andalusian (above) owes its origins to the Barb. It is an elegant riding horse, and you can see them striding along in Spanish ceremonial processions at the *ferias*, or fairs. Usually bays or greys, they are up to 15.2 hands and provide an active, attractive ride.

Inspired in part by the wealth of Wild West dramas at the cinema, riders in many parts of the world have taken up Western riding. It is practical and fun. Leather chaps are worn instead of breeches and boots, and the big Western saddle is comfortable to sit in for long rides on the flat, but it is not an ideal jumping saddle.

The Missouri Fox-trotting horse (above) was bred to cover long distances over bad going while providing a comfortable ride.

The speedy combination on the right is taking part in barrel racing, where competitors race between and around barrels laid out in a pattern. Modern riding experts have one criticism of Western riding: the ten-gallon hat is anything but safe if you fall on your head.

CLASSICS

One of the special delights of the horse world: Camargue horses, owing their name to their homeland in the marsh region at the mouth of the Rhône in southern France. Known as the 'wild white horses of the sea', they were kept as mounts by the *gardiens*, the herdsmen who work the black fighting bulls of the Camargue. A group of *gardiens* is seen below.

The Camargue horse may have ancient connections with the Barb. It was only as recently as 1968 that the Camargue was officially recognized as a separate breed. Nowadays a famous conservation area in Europe, the Camargue is a favourite tourist spot, and visitors may ride Camargue horses to view the abundant wildlife of this ancient marshland.

One of the glories of Austria, and a must for every horse-lover, is the Spanish Riding School in Vienna. Its famous Lipizzaner horses are bred at Piber, near Graz in Upper Styria, and you can see the mares and foals there on conducted visits. Its relaxed rural setting is a contrast with the splendour of the early 18th-century riding hall at the Imperial Palace in Vienna, used by the Spanish Riding School since the reign of Emperor Charles VI. Only the Lipizzaner stallions perform the famous high-school movements in the school. Why Spanish? The horses were imported from Spain to a stud at Lipizza, near Trieste, where the breed was founded to perform the exquisite high-school movements which we can still enjoy today. Its riders train for years to achieve classical equitation movements. This is where equestrianism and art combine.

One of the most exciting aspects of the high-school displays by Lipizzaners is their ability to explode into amazing leaps, known as 'airs above the ground'. The *ballotade* (shown above) is performed in hand. The stallion is almost parallel to the ground when at the summit of its leap. The Spanish Riding School stallions work in hand at the difficult movements before they perform them with riders. During the Spanish Riding School display (left) a stallion performs the *piaffe*, a trot on the spot, between pillars which derive from classical riding training methods.
Since the Second World War the Spanish Riding School has made numerous tours, and has millions of admirers all over the world.

THE CHASE

It is a rare sight in the modern hunting field, but side-saddle riding is practical over large fences. Ladies were not especially welcome in the hunting field until the latter part of the last century, and their participation was helped by the invention of the 'safety skirt' which helps to prevent the rider becoming disastrously tangled with the horse if the mount should fall. In the show ring (above) it is still correct to wear a full side-saddle habit, and to use the side-saddle, in ladies' show hunter classes. Although there has been some revival in this style, the vast majority of girls start riding astride, and never aspire to the expense, time and trouble involved in side-saddle riding despite its undoubted appeal in sheer elegance.

Fox-hunting remains the largest participant riding sport in Britain, with over 200 registered hunts providing sport for over 50,000 people riding regularly to hounds, and many more appearing occasionally among the mounted followers. Those who hunt in Leicestershire with the Quorn (left) usually change to a fresh horse halfway through a day of galloping over old turf, and jumping cut-and-laid fences. This is the 'capital' of hunting, but it flourishes wherever there is huntable land.

'Happy is he who goes out to please himself, and not to h'astonish others', was the dictum of the great sporting character Jorrocks, created by Surtees. Part of the attraction of the chase, still difficult to convey to those who do not hunt, is the feeling of freedom which it bestows on the followers, who vary in age from young children to some in their eighties. The sport is enjoyed on ponies, old cobs or high-couraged blood hunters. It simply depends on the type of country you expect to cross.

After the huntsman has blown for home with his hunting horn, the mounted field wend their way from the 'Elysian Fields' of high Leicestershire. Fox-hunting with the Quorn Hunt, founded in 1753, still attracts up to 150 riders on its most popular days, Mondays and Fridays, during a long season from November to mid-March. The large enclosures allow the riders to jump as many as 50 abreast in the best of the country. In Gloucestershire the premier pack is the Duke of Beaufort's (below) where the huntsman and whippers-in wear dark green hunt coats instead of the red coats sported by hunt staffs in most other packs. The Duke of Beaufort's subscribers mainly wear blue hunt coats with buff facings.

Such traditions are strong, and despite the opposition, hunting survives because it copes remarkably well with modern changes in the countryside, and draws its support from the widest possible cross-section of society.

Handsome Heavyweights

The grandeur of the Shire horse in the show ring is
something people take for granted, yet this marvellous
breed was nearly lost after the Second World War.
Increased mechanization on farms caused a huge drop
in the number of pure-bred Shire horses left in Britain.
Sterling work by a handful of enthusiasts in the Shire
Horse Society saved the breed. This was aided by a
greatly-increased export market in young Shire horses
to North America. Derbyshire is especially noted as a
county where many farmers still breed Shire horses as
a side-line to sheep and cattle farming.
The team of four (above) are pulling a harrow and the
pair on the right are seen parading at a show.

Overleaf: A pair of Clydesdales ploughing.

Happiness in Harness

Exotic, dashing and with irresistible reminders of great Russian dramas . . . a troika of Orlov Trotters. They evoke scenes of escape across the snow, with wolves howling in pursuit. This Russian breed owes its name to Count Alexis Grigorievich Orlov, who cross-bred a white Arab stallion, Smetanka, with Thoroughbred and other mares to produce these exciting grey horses. The breed nowadays contains five distinct types, of which the most typical is the medium-sized Khrenov. They were originally produced at the Orlov Stud, near Moscow. A troika, a Russian term for a team of three horses driven abreast, is drawing a four-wheeled open carriage called a calèche.

There are many ways of driving horses and ponies in harness, and here is a transatlantic contrast. On the left, one of Britain's leading drivers, Mrs Cynthia Haydon, shows off a Hackney pony to perfection in the show ring. The Hackney horse and pony are notable for their showy trot with high-knee action. They are volatile animals and need considerable skill in driving and handling. The foreleg has to stride well forward as well as up, so that the Hackney appears to float over the ground. Above, at Tampa, Florida, a trotter is driven in the light two-wheeled cart called a sulky. This vehicle is also used to drive pacers, which, instead of trotting with the usual diagonal action, move with the fore and hind legs together on the same side. Trotting and pacing racing is very popular in many countries.

Overleaf: A pair going through the water obstacle in the carriage-driving contest at the Royal Windsor Horse Show.

Switzerland's famous ski resort, St Moritz, has an attraction which surprises many visitors: horse sports on its frozen lake. The Swiss have devised special non-slip horseshoes, using rubber as well as metal, which enable horses to perform at all speeds on the snow-covered ice. They play polo, they show-jump and, as seen here, they hold trotting races. It is just one more remarkable demonstration of the versatility of our four-legged friends. Provided they are well rugged-up when they are not working, the horses suffer no ill effects from the freezing temperatures. It is the spectators who find horse sports on ice something of an ordeal, and they are usually fortified with hot mulled wine.

CHALLENGE ON THE TURF

Jockeyship is all about timing and the will to win, as well as the equestrian skill which can forge a partnership with a horse the very first time the rider sits on its back. Everything the jockey does is watched more closely than ever before, thanks to television cameras. The stewards are closely on the look-out for such offences as bumping, or obstructing other horses unfairly, and they take more trouble nowadays to ensure that a jockey does not use the whip harshly. A great deal can be achieved in the vital run-up to the winning post by flourishing the whip without striking the horse. Fines and suspensions are the penalties handed out impartially to famous jockeys or novices if the stewards think the rules of racing have been broken. Sometimes their justice seems tough – but it is good for the health of racing, and for the welfare of our remarkable friend, the horse.

Overleaf: Exercising
Following page: Racing on an all-weather course.

The great winter sport of National Hunt racing offers amateur riders far more scope than Flat racing in the summer months, which is more heavily dominated by professional jockeys. Amateurs ride against professionals in many jump races, and amateurs have their own hunter 'chase races too. Hurdling, seen above, produces big fields because a great many horses are diverted from flat racing to this sport. Finding top-class steeplechasers to take on the big obstacles, such as the water jump (right) is far more difficult. Fortunately, a top-class steeplechaser tends to stay in the public eye for more than a few seasons and becomes a national hero.

THE GREAT GAME

One of the oldest and fastest sports in the world, polo flourishes in most equestrian countries. It is an ancient sport – the Persians were playing in 500 BC – but its appeal is as strong as ever. The polo pony is usually a horse, since it measures well above 14.2 hands. Most players agree that the best polo ponies come from South America, especially from Argentina. They are extraordinarily agile, having amazing powers of acceleration, can make sudden changes of direction, and the best exhibit well-above-average equine intelligence.

High-goal polo is so named because its players, in teams of four, bear handicaps, from minus two to ten in ascending order of merit. They have to hit the ball between goal posts to score, but each time they score they change ends – which is confusing for a new spectator. Play is divided into periods of seven minutes each, called chukkas. Since each player needs a fresh pony for each new chukka, it is a sport which calls for a deep purse as well as immense enthusiasm. High-goal polo teams are usually sponsored by wealthy patrons who fill their teams with professional players, many of them going from South America to Europe for the summer season.

Polo ponies need courage to withstand aggressive 'riding off', which is the way one player can gain possession of the ball from another. Striking the ball accurately at speed requires hours of practice, which starts from the back of a wooden horse. Then stick and ball practice from horseback follows, and has to be maintained throughout the rider's career. Positional play is vital in polo. A brilliant individual is important, but he must also exhibit the virtues of a real team player.

Complete Horsemanship

Dressage is still a growing sport at all levels. Dr Reiner Klimke, the West German Olympic gold medallist dressage rider, and his renowned horse Ahlerich (left) show the discipline combined with sheer artistry needed to win world-class competitions. Judges award marks for each movement in a dressage test, and at international level there are between 30 and 40 such movements. West Germany has dominated the dressage scene in the postwar years, but enthusiasm is immense in many countries. The spotted horse (above) is performing in front of Blenheim Palace, the Oxfordshire home of the Duke and Duchess of Marlborough.

S ince the sport of horse trials, or eventing, seeks to be the complete test of a riding horse, a basic dressage test is the first phase of its rigorous competition. Two competitors from the United States and Britain in the Seoul Olympic Games show their paces: Phyllis Dawson (U.S. above), and Virginia Leng (G.B. right) on Nightcap. Virginia is a former world champion dressage rider, and displays remarkable accuracy in riding in all three phases of the three-day event: dressage, cross-country riding and show-jumping. Hours of hard work in training and a true partnership with the horse are required in eventing, which is such a tough sport that women riders were banned from competing at Olympic level until 1956. Now they take on the best in the world.

One of the great days in the equestrian calendar: the cross-country phase at Badminton Horse Trials in Britain, held annually in the spring. Huge crowds of more than 250,000 flock to the park around Badminton House, home of the Duke and Duchess of Beaufort, in the county of Avon. The founding of this event by the 10th Duke in 1949 made a huge contribution to the standards achieved in this sport in Britain, enabling British riders to win more Olympic medals, and world and European championships, than in any other horse sport in the postwar years.

Badminton is still an imposing challenge, where the aim of the course builder is to erect obstacles which 'frighten the riders, but do not harm the horses'. Badminton's lake (below) is incorporated in a spectacular series of daring jumps which attracts the largest group of spectators on the course. Ian Stark is seen (top right) jumping into the Badminton lake on Murphy Himself, the exuberant grey horse with which he won the world championship individual silver medal at Stockholm in 1990.

Courage is a major factor in eventing, as shown here by the Dutch rider Eddy Stibbe on Bristol's Autumn Spirit II at the Badminton Horse Trials. The horse is a gregarious animal which likes to perform in groups, but the event horse has to produce its best form when going round a course on its own, without other horses giving a lead or helping to increase its confidence, as happens in racing. Although this spread over water in front of solid timber is demanding, it should be remembered that the scope of a large horse in jumping spreads is enormous. Even if taking off from a standstill it can clear up to 5.5m (18 ft). For the rider the aim is to keep the horse well balanced before each take-off, and to maintain a relentless, ground-devouring stride at an even tempo in the galloping between each cross-country fence.

Riding across country in a three-day event involves beating the clock as well as completing the course without refusals or falls. So Karen Straker (above), one of Britain's world championship and Olympic team members, wears a large watch to enable her to check her time throughout the course so that she can avoid picking up time penalties. The riders walk the course frequently beforehand to work out timing, as well as to decide on the best places to tackle each obstacle.

As can be seen at the Burghley Horse Trials (opposite), there is not much margin for error when tackling a fence such as this: a bullfinch with a water ditch in front. The horse must jump boldly through the top of the bullfinch, which derives from the uncut hedge met in the hunting field. The maxim which is vital in all forms of jumping formidable obstacles is: 'Throw your heart over first.'

LEAPING TO GLORY

Show-jumping demands ice-cool nerves, superb accuracy and a truly exceptional horse if you are to win at world level. John Whitaker and the superb grey gelding Henderson Milton (left) fill the bill exactly, as they have shown in so many international contests. Milton's fans send him Christmas cards and demand hairs from his tail as souvenirs. He is one of the most popular horses in the history of show jumping.

In Britain the best outdoor setting for the sport is the All England Jumping Course, at Hickstead in Sussex (below). It was founded and developed by the dedicated show jumping enthusiast Douglas Bunn. The major annual attraction there is the famous Jumping Derby.

Leading American rider Anne Kursinski and Starman demonstrate why show-jumping attracts huge audiences in stadiums and on worldwide satellite television. Courses have become far more varied in the postwar years, such as the water obstacle at Aachen (opposite). Some people fear that courses are too demanding nowadays, but show-jumping horses have a remarkable record of high achievement at ages in their late teens which would be considered geriatric in endurance sports such as eventing or steeplechasing. Show-jumping riders are great survivors too, often continuing to stay at the top of their sport in their fifties. Show-jumping can rob a partnership of victory by mere fractions of a second in timing, or the slightest mistake in lowering a fence. It is nerve-racking but it is nothing like as stressful for the horse as high-speed work.

Our partnership with the horse, as we have seen, takes an amazing variety of forms. In all sports and activities, however, it has to be just that to achieve anything worthwhile: a meaningful partnership. Let's call it true friendship.

Acknowledgements

Action-Plus Photographic/Chris Barry 70–71,/Mike Hewitt 68–69, 72;
Animal Photography/Sally Anne Thompson 20–21, 28–29, 29, 32, 42
inset, 58–59, 60–61, 61,/R Willbie 54, 78–79; Austrian National Tourist
Office 45; Robert Harding Picture Library 42–43; Kit Houghton 1, 2,
6–7, 8, 9, 10, 14–15, 16–17, 18, 21, 24–25, 25, 33, 34, 38, 40–41, 49, 52,
52–53, 55, 64–65, 76, 84–85, 85 inset, 88, 90–91; Bob Langrish 11, 19,
22–23, 26, 27, 30–31, 36–37, 37, 38–39, 44, 48–49, 50 inset,
50–51, 56–57, 62–63, 66–67, 72–73, 74–75, 77, 80, 81, 82, 83, 89, 90
inset, 92–93, 94, 95; Sandra Langrish 86–87; Trevor Meeks 46; Octopus
Publishing Group Ltd/Kit Houghton 4–5; Elisabeth Weiland 35, 47;
ZEFA Picture Library 12–13.